Great Americana

A Brief Description of New-York

Daniel Denton

A Brief
Description of
New-York

by Daniel Denton

READEX MICROPRINT

Foreword

A Brief Description of New-York: Formerly Called New-Netherlands was written by Daniel Denton and published in London in 1670. Denton's *Description* provided English readers with their first close look at a colony which only a few years before had belonged to the Dutch. The author hoped to arouse interest in New York and to encourage English emigration to it.

In March, 1664, Charles II had granted to his brother James, Duke of York, proprietorship over the territory which lay between the Connecticut River and Delaware Bay. However, since the Dutch had for some years occupied and governed that same territory under the name "New Netherland," the land grant to James meant nothing unless he could break the Dutch hold. Despite the peace which then existed between England and Holland, an English fleet was dispatched to New Netherland to enforce the claim. The Dutch surrendered in September, 1664, and the colony of some six to ten thousand persons came under English rule. To insure English domination, as well as profitable development of the newly acquired colony, substantial numbers of English settlers were urgently required.

Although the Indians and the Dutch had talked of precious stones and metals to be found in New York, Denton disdained such reports and, with disarming frankness, told his readers, "I shall not feed your expectation with any thing of that nature." Instead, Denton preferred to discuss the more conventional, but still very valuable, resources of the country. The territory contained many fur-bearing animals, rich stands of timber, well-stocked streams, and fertile lands capable of a variety of agricultural uses.

The author explained the manner in which companies might be organized to settle the new lands, advised the emigrants what to bring with them for settlement in New York, and wrote in glowing terms of the economic opportunities which awaited. New York, he thought, could support a large population. Persons settling there could, "with Gods blessing, and their own industry, live as happily as any people in the world." For the benefit of those who might hesitate to emigrate through fear of the Indians, Denton had some reassuring words. "It hath been generally observed," he wrote, "that where the English come to settle, a Divine Hand makes way for them, by removing or cutting off the Indians, either by Wars one with the other, or by some raging mortal Disease."

Felix Neumann has supplied additional information about the book in his introduction to Daniel Denton, *A Brief Description of New York* (Cleveland, 1902), pp. 5-32.

A

Brief Description

O F

NEW-YORK:

Formerly Called

New-Netherlands

With the Places thereunto Adjoyning.

Together with the

Manner of its Scituation, Fertility of the Soyle,
Healthfulneſs of the Climate, and the
Commodities thence produced.

ALSO

Some Directions and Advice to ſuch as ſhall go
thither: An Account of what Commodities they ſhall
take with them; The Profit and Pleaſure that
may acciew to them thereby.

LIKEWISE

A Brief RELATION of the Cuſtoms of the
Indians there.

By *DANIEL DENTON.*

LONDON,

TO THE

Reader.

Reader,

I Have here thorough the Instigation of divers Persons in *England*, and elsewhere, presented you with a Brief but true Relation of a known unknown part of *America*. The known part which is either inhabited, or lieth near the Sea, I have described to you, and have writ nothing, but what I have been an eye-witness to all or the greatest part of it : Neither can I safely say, was I willing to exceed, but was rather willing the place it self should exceed my Commendation, which *I* question not but will be owned by those that shall travel

A 3   thither :

thither : For the unknown part, which is either some places lying to the Northward yet undiscovered by any *English*, or the Bowels of the earth not yet opened, though the Natives tell us of Glittering Stones, Diamonds, or Pearl in the one, and the *Dutch* hath boasted of Gold and Silver in the o ther ; yet I shall not feed your expecta- tion with any thing of that nature ; but leave it til a better discovery shal I make way for such a Relation. In the mean time accept of this from him who desi- reth to deal impartially with every one,

DANIEL DENTON.

A

A
Brief Relation

O F
N E W Y O R K,

With the Plces thereunto Adjoyning, fornely called

THE NEW NETHERLANDS, &c.

That Tract of Land formerly called *The New Nethe lands*, doth Contain all that Land which lieth in the North parts of *America*, betwixt *New-England* and *May-Land* in *Virginia*, the length of which Northward into the Countrey, as it hath not been fully discovered, so it is not certainly known The bredth of it is about two hundred miles: The principal Rivers within this Tract, are *Hal sons* River, *Raritan*-River, and *Delewerbay*-River. The chief Islands are the *Manahatans*-Island, *Long*-Island, and *Staten*-Island.

And

And first to begin with the *Manahatans* Island, so
called by the *Indians*, it lieth within land betwixt the
degrees of 41. and 42. of North-latitude, and is a-
bout 14 miles long, and two broad. It is bounded
with *Long*-Island on the South, with *Staten*-Island on
the West, on the North with the Main Land: And with
Conecticut Colony on the East-side of it; only a part
of the Main Land belonging to *New-York* Colony,
where several Towns and Villages are setled, being
about thirty miles in bredth, doth intercept the *Manahatans* Island, and the Colony of *Conecticut* before. mentioned.

New-York is setled upon the West-end of the a-
foresaid Island, having that small arm of the Sea,
which divides it from *Long*-Island on the South side
of it, which runs away Eastward to *New-England*,
and is Navigable, though dangerous. For about ten
miles from *New-York* is a place called *Hell-Gate*,
which being a narrow passage, there runneth a vio-
lent stream both upon flood and ebb, and in the
middle lieth some Islands of Rocks, which the Cur-
rent sets so violently upon, that it threatens present
shipwrack; and upon the Flood is a large Whirl-
pool, which continually sends forth a hideous roar-
ing, enough to affright any stranger from passing
further, and to wait for some *Charon* to conduct
him thorough; yet to those that are well acquainted
little or no danger; yet a place of great defence a-
ga nst any enemy coming in that way, which a small
Fortification would absolutely prevent, and neces-
sitate them to come in at the West end of *Long*-I-
sland by *Sandy Hook*, where *Nutten*-Island doth force
them within Command of the Fort at *New York*,
which is one of the best Pieces of Defence in the
North-parts of *America*.

New

New York is built moſt of Brick and Stone, and covered with red and black Tile, and the Land being high, it gives at a diſtance a p'eaſing Aſpect to the ſpectators. The Inhabitants conſiſt moſt of *Engliſh* and *Dutch*, and have a conſiderable Trade with the *Indians*, for *Bevers, Otter, Raccoon* skins, with other Furrs; As alſo for *Bear, Deers*, and *Elke* skins; and are ſupplied with Veniſon and Fowl in the Winter, and Fiſh in the Summer by the *Indians*, which they buy at an eaſie rate; And having the Countrey round about them, they are continually furniſhed with all ſuch proviſions as is needful for the life of man; not only by the *Engliſh* and *Dutch* within their own, but likewiſe by the Adjacent Colonies.

The Commodities vented from thence is Furs and Skins before-mentioned; As likewiſe *Tobacco* made within the Colony, as good as is uſually made in *Mary-land*: Alſo *Horſes, Beef, Pork, Oyl, Peiſe, Wheat*, and the like.

Long-Iſland, the Weſt-end of which lies Southward of *New-York*, runs Eaſtward above one hundred miles, and is in ſome places eight, in ſome twelve, in ſome fourteen miles broad; it is inhabited from one end to the other. On the Weſt end is four or five *Dutch* Towns, the reſt being all *Engliſh* to the number of twelve, beſides Villages and Farm houſes. The Iſland is moſt of it of a very good ſoyle, and very natural for all ſorts of *Engliſh* Grain; which they ſowe and have very good increaſe of, beſides all other Fruits and Herbs common in *England*, as alſo *Tobacco*, *Hemp*, *Flax*, *Pumpkies, Melons*, &c.

The Fruits natural to the Iſland, are *Mullerries, Poſimons*,

B

Posimons, *Grapes* great and small, *Huckelberries,* *Cramberries,* *Plums* of several sorts, *Rosberries* and *Strawberries,* of which last is such abundance in *June,* that the Fields and Woods are died red: Which the Countrey-people perceiving, instantly arm themselves with bottles of Wine, Cream, and Sugar, and in sted of a Coat of Male, every one takes a Female upon his Horse behind him, and so rushing violently into the fields, never leave till they have disrob'd them of their red colours, and turned them into the old habit.

The greatest part of the Island is very full of Timber, as Oaks white and red, Walnut-trees, Chesnut-trees, which yield store of Mast for Swine, and are often therewith sufficiently fatted with Oat-Corn: as also Maples, Cedars, Saxifrage, Beach, Birch, Holly, Hazel, with many sorts more.

The Herbs which the Countrey naturally afford, are Purslain, white Orage, Egrimony, Violets, Penniroyal, Alicampane, besides Saxaparilla very common, with many more. Yea, in *May* you shall see the Woods and Fields so curiously bedecke with Roses, and an innumerable multitude of delightful Flowers, not only pleasing the eye, but smell, that you may behold Nature contending with Art, and striving to equal, if not excel many Gardens in *England*: nay, did we know the vertue of all those Plants and Herbs growing there (which time may more discover) many are of opinion, and the Natives do affirm, that there is no disease common to the Countrey, but may be cured without Materials from other Nations.

There is several Navigable Rivers and Bays, which
puts

puts into the North-side of *Long*-Islan^d, but upon the South-side which joyns to the Sea, it is so fortified with bars of sands and sholes, that it is a sufficient defence against any enemy, yet the South-side is not without Brooks and Riverets, which empty themselves into the Sea ; yea, you shall scarce travel a mile, but you shall meet with one of them whose Christal streams run so swift, that they purge themselves of such stinking mud and filth, which the standing or low-paced streams of most brooks and rivers westward of this Colony leave lying, and are by the Suns exhalation dissipated, the Air corrupted, and many Fevers and other distempers occasioned, not incident to this Colony : Neither do the Brooks and Riverets premised, give way to the Frost in Winter, or draught in Summer, but keep their course throughout the year.

These Rivers are very well furnished with Fish, as Bosse, Sheepsheads, Place, Pearch, Trouts, Eels, Turtles, and divers others.

The Island is plentifully stored with all sorts of *English* Cattel. Horses, Hogs, Sheep, Goats, &c. no place in the North of *America* better, which they can both raise and maintain, by reason of the large and spacious Medows or Marches wherewith it is furnished, the Island likewise producing excellent *English* grass, the seed of which was brought out of *England*, which they sometime mow twice a year.

For wilde Beasts there is Deer, Bear, Wolves, Foxes, Racoons, Otters, Musquashes and Skunks. Wild Fowl there is great store of, as Turkies, Heath-Hens, Quailes, Partridges, Pidgeons, Cranes, Geese

of

of several forts, Brants, Ducks, Widgeon, Teal, and
divers others: There is also the red Bird, with divers forts of finging birds, whose chirping notes fa-
lute the ears of Travellers with an harmonious dif-
cord, and in every pond and brook green filken
Frogs, who warbling forth their untun'd tunes
firive to bear a part in this mufick.

Towards the middle of Long-Ifland lyeth a plain
fixteen miles long and four broad, upon which
plain grows very fine grafs, that makes exceeding
good Hay, and is very good pafture for fheep or o-
ther Cattel; where you fhall find neither flick nor
ftone to hinder the Horfe heels, or endanger them
in their Races, and once a year the beft Horfes in the
Ifland are brought hither to try their fwiftnefs, and
the fwifteft rewarded with a filver Cup. two being
Annually procured for that purpofe. There are two
or three other fmall plains of about a mile fquare,
which are no fmall benefit to thofe Towns which
enjoy them.

Upon the South-fide of Long-Ifland in the Winter, lie ftore of Whales and Crampaffes, which the
inhabitants begin with fmall boats to make a trade
Catching to their no fmall benefit. Alfo an innu_
merable multitude of Seals, which make an excellent oyle; they lie all the Winter upon fome broken
Marfhes and Beaches, or bars of fand before-mentioned, and might be eafily got were there fome fkilful
men would undertake it.

To fay fomething of the Indians, there is now but
few upon the Ifland, and thofe few no ways hurtful
but rather ferviceable to the English, and it is to be
admired, how ftrangely they have deereaft by the
Hand

Hand of God, since the *English* first setling of those parts; for since my time, where there we e six towns, they are reduced to two small Villages, and it hath been generally observed, that where the *English* come to settle, a Divine Hand makes way for them, by removing or cutting off the *Indians*, either by Wars one with the other, or by some raging mortal Disease.

They live principally by Hunting, Fowling, and Fishing: their Wives being the Husbandmen to till the Land, and plant their corn.

The meat they live most upon is Fish, Fowl, and Venison; they eat likewise Polecats, Skunks, Racoon, Possum, Turtles, and the like.

They build small moveable Tents, which they remove two or three times a year, having their principal quarters where they plant their Corn: their Hunting quarters, and their Fishing quarters: Their Recreations are chiefly Foot-ball and Cards, at which they will play away all they have, excepting a Flap to cover their nakedness: They are great lovers of strong drink, yet do not care for drinking, unless they have enough to make themselves drunk; and if there be so many in their Company, that there is not sufficient to make them all drunk, they usually select so many out of their Company, proportionable to the quantity of drink, and the rest must be Spectators. And if any one chance to be drunk before he hath finisht his proportion, (which is ordinarily a quart of Brandy, Rum or Strong-waters) the rest will pour the rest of his part down his throat.

They

They often kill one another at these drunken Matches, which the friends of the murdered person, do revenge upon the Murderer unless he purchase his life with money, which they sometimes do: Their money is made of a Periwinkle shell of which there is black and white, made much like unto beads, and put upon strings.

For their worship which is diabolical, it is performed usually but once or twice a-year, unless upon some extraordinary occasion, as upon making of War or the like; their usual time is about *Michaelmass*, when their corn is first ripe, the day being appointed by their chief Priest or pawaw; most of them go a hunting for venison: When they are all congregated, their priest tells them if he want money, there God will accept of no other offering, which the people beleeving, every one gives money according to their ability. The priest takes the money, and putting it into some dishes, sets them upon the top of their low flat-roofed houses, and falls to invocating their God to come and receive it, which with a many loud hallows and outcries, knocking the ground with sticks, and beating themselves, is performed by the priest, and seconded by the people.

After they have thus a while wearied themselves, the priest by his Conjuration brings in a devil amongst them, in the shape sometimes of a fowl, sometimes of a beast, and somtimes of a man, at which the people being amazed, not daring to stir, he improves the opportunity, steps out, and makes sure of the money, and then returns to lay the spirit, who in the mean time is sometimes gone, and takes some of the Company along with him: but if any *English* at such times do come amongst them, it puts
a pe-

a period to their proceeding, and they will defire their abfence, telling them their God will not come whilft they are there.

In their wars they fight no pitcht fields, but when they have notice of an enemies approach, they endeavor to fecure their wives and children upon fome Ifland, or in fome thick fwamp, and then with their guns and hatchets they way-lay their enemies, fome lying behind one, fome another, and it is a great fight where feven or eight is flain.

When any *Indian* dies amongft them, they bury him upright, fitting upon a feat, with his Gun, money, and fuch goods as he hath with him, that he may be furnifhed in the other world, which they conceive is Weftward, where they fhall have great ftore of Game for Hunting and live eafie lives. At his Burial his neareft Relations attend the Hearfe with their faces painted black, and do vifit the grave once or twice a day, where they fend forth fad lamentations fo long, till time hath wore the blacknefs off their faces; and afterwards every year once they view the grave, make a new mourning for him, trimming up of the Grave, not fuffering of a Grafs to grow by it: they fence their graves with a hedge, and cover the tops with Mats, to fhelter them from the rain.

Any *Indian* being dead, his Name dies with him, no perfon daring ever after to mention his Name, it being not only a breach of their Law, but an abufe to his friends and relations prefent, as if it were done on purpofe to renew their grief: And any other perfon whatfoever that is named after that name doth incontinently change his name, and
takes

takes a new one, their names are not proper set names as among ſtChriſtians, but every one invents a name to himſelf, which he likes beſt. Some calling themſelves *Ra tle-ſnake*, *Skunk*, *Bucks-horn*, or the like: And if a perſon die, that his name is ſome word which is uſed in ſpeech, they likewiſe change that word, and invent ſome new one, which makes a great change and alteration in their language.

When any perſon is ſick, after ſome means uſed by his friends, every one pretending ſkill in Phyſick; that proving ineffectual, they ſend for a Pawaw or Prieſt, who ſitting down by the ſick perſon, without the leaſt enquiry after the diſtemper, waits for a gift, which he proportions his work accordingly to: that being received, he firſt begins with a low voice to call upon his God, calling ſometimes upon one, ſometimes on another, raiſing his voice higher and higher, beating of his naked breaſts and ſides, till the ſweat runneth down, and his breath is almoſt gone, then that little which is remaining, he evaporates upon the face of the ſick perſon three or four times together, and ſo takes his leave.

Their Marriages are performed without any Ceremony, the Match being firſt made by money. The ſum being agreed upon and given to the woman, it makes a conſummation of their Marriage, if I may ſo call it: After that, he keeps her during his pleaſure, and upon the leaſt diſlike turns her away and takes another: It is no offence for their married women to lie with another man, provided ſhe acquaint her husband, or ſome of her neareſt Relations with it, but if not, it is accounted ſuch a fault that they ſometimes puniſh it with death: An *Indian* may have two wives or more if he pleaſe; but t is not ſo much in uſe as it was ſince the *Engliſh* came amongſt them: they being ready in ſome meaſure
ſure

sure to imitate the *English* in things both good and bad: any Maid before she is married doth lie with whom she please for money, without any scandal, or the least aspersion to be cast upon her, it being so customary, and their laws tolerating of it. They are extraordinary charitable one to another, one having nothing to spare, but he freely imparts it to his friends, and whatsoever they get by gaming or any other way, they share one to another, leaving themselves commonly the least share.

At their *Cantica's* or dancing Matches, where all persons that come are freely entertain'd, it being a Festival time: Their custom is when they dance, every one but the Dancers to have a short stick in their hand, and to knock the ground and sing altogether, whilst they that dance sometimes act warlike postures, and then they come in painted for War with their faces black and red, or some all black, some all red, with some streaks of white under their eyes, and so jump and leap up and down without any order, uttering many expressions of their intended valour. For other Dances they only shew what Antick tricks their ignorance will lead them to, wringing of their bodies and faces after a strange manner, sometimes jumping into the fire, sometimes catching up a Fire-brand, and biting off a live coal, with many such tricks, that will affright, if not please an *English* man to look upon them, resembling rather a company of infernal Furies then men. When their King or *Sachem* sits in Council, he hath a Company of armed men to guard his Person, great respect being shewen him by the People, which is principally manifested by their silence: After he hath declared the cause of their convention, he demands their opinion, ordering who shall begin: The person ordered to speak, after he hath declared his minde, tells them he hath

C   done:

done : no man ever interrupting any person in his speech, nor offering to speak, though he make never so many or long stops, till he says he hath no more to say : the Council having all declar'd their opinions, the King after some pause gives the definitive sentence, which is commonly seconded with a shout from the people, every one seeming to applaud, and manifest their Assent to what is determined : If any person be condemned to die, which is seldom, unless for Murder or Incest, the King himself goes out in person (for you must understand they have no prisons, and the guilty person flies into the Woods) where they go in quest of him, and having found him, the King shoots first, though at never such a distance, and then happy is the man can shoot him down, and cut off his *Long*, which they commonly wear, who for his pains is made some Captain, or other military Officer.

Their Cloathing is a yard and an half of broad Cloth, which is made for the *Indian* Trade, which they hang upon their shoulders ; and half a yard of the same cloth, which being put betwixt their legs, and brought up before and behinde, and tied with a Girdle about their middle, hangs with a flap on each side : They wear no Hats, but commonly wear about their Heads a Snake's skin, or a Belt of their money, or a kind of a Ruff made with Deers hair, and died of a scarlet colour, which they esteem very rich.

They grease their bodies and hair very often, and paint their faces with several colours, as black, white, red, yellow, blew, &c. which they take great pride in, every one being painted in a several manner : Thus much for the Customs of the *Indians*.

Within.

Within two Leagues of *New-York* lieth *Staten-Island*, it bears from *New York* West something Southerly : It is about twenty miles long, and four or five broad; it is moſt of it very good Land, full of Timber, and produceth all ſuch commodities as Long-*Iſland* doth, beſides Tin and ſtore of Iron Oar, and the Calamine ſtone is ſaid likewiſe to be found there : There is but one Town upon it conſiſting of *Engliſh* and *French*, but is capable of entertaining more Inhabitants : betwixt this and Long *Iſland* is a large Bay, and is the coming in for all ſhips and veſſels out of the Sea : On the North-ſide of this Iſland *After-skull* River puts into the main Land on the Weſt-ſide, whereof is two or three Towns, but on the Eaſt-ſide but one. There is very great Marſhes or Medows on both ſides of it, excellent good Land, an good conveniencefor the ſetling of ſeveral Towns; there grows black Walnut and Locuſt, as their doth in *Virginia*, with mighty tall ſtreight Timber, as good as any in the North of *America* : It produceth any Commoditie *Long-Iſland* doth.

Hudſons River runs by *New-York* Northward into the Countrey, toward the Head of which is ſeated *New-Albany*, a place of great Trade with the *Indians*, betwixt which and *New-York*, being above one hundred miles, is as good Corn-land as the World affords, enough to entertain Hundreds of Families, which in the time of the *Dutch*-Government of thoſe parts could not be ſetled: For the *Indians*, excepting one place, called the Sters, which was kept by a Garriſon, but ſince the reducement of thoſe parts under His Maⁱeſties obedience, and a Patent granted to his Royal Highneſs the Duke of *York*, which is about ſix years ; ſince by the care and diligence of the Honourable

Coll.

Coll. *Nichol's* sent thither Deputy to His Highness, such a League of Peace was made, and Friendship concluded betwixt that Colony and the *Indians*, that they have not resisted or disturbed any Christians there, in the setling or peaceable possessing of any Lands with that Government, but every man hath sate under his own Vine, and hath peaceably reapt and enjoyed the fruits of their own labours, which God continue.

Westward of *After-Kull* River before mentioned, about 18 or 20 miles runs in *Raritan*-River Northward into the Countrey, some score of miles, both sides of which River is adorn'd with spacious Medows, enough to maintain thousands of Cattel, the Wood-land is likewise very good for corn, and stor'd with wilde Beasts, as Deer, and Elks, and an innumerable multitude of Fowl, as in other parts of the Countrey: This River is thought very capable for the erecting of several Towns and Villages on each side of it, no place in the North of *America* having better convenience for the maintaining of all sorts of Cattel for Winter and Summer-food: upon this River is no town setled, but one at the mouth of it. Next this River Westward is a place called *New-asons*, where is two or three Towns and Villages setled upon the Sea-side, but none betwixt that and *Delewer* Bay, which is about sixty miles, all which is a rich Champain Countrey, free from stones, and indifferent level; store of excellent good timber, and very well watered, having brooks or rivers ordinarily, one or more in every miles travel: The Countrey is full of Deer, Elks, Bear, and other Creatures, as in other parts of the Countrey, where you shall meet with no inhabitant in this journey, but a few *Indians*, where there is stately Oaks, whose broad-branched-tops serve for no other use, but to

keep

keep off the Suns heat from the wilde Beasts of the Wilderneſs, where is graſs as high as a mans middle, that ſerves for no other end except to maintain the Elks and Deer, who never devour a huudredth part of it, then to be burnt every Spring to make way for new. How many poor people in the world would think themſelves happy, had they an Acre or two of Land, whilſt here is hundreds, nay thouſands of Acres, that would invite inhabitants.

Delewerba the mouth of the River, lyeth about the Mid-way betwixt *New-York* and the *Capes* of *Virginia* : It is a very pleaſant River and Countrey, but very few inhabitants, and them being moſtly *Swedes*, *Dutch* and *Finns* : about ſixty miles up the River is the principal Town called *New-Caſtle*, which is about 40 miles from *Mary-land*, and very good way to travel either with horſe or foot, the people are ſetled all along the weſt ſide ſixty miles above *New-Caſtle*; the land is good for all ſorts of *Engliſh* grain, and wanteth nothing but a good people to populate it, it being capable of entertaining many hundred families.

Some may admire, that theſe great and rich Tracts of land, lying ſo adjoyning to *New-England* and *Virginia* ſhould be no better inhabited, and that the richneſs of the ſoyle, the healthfulneſs of the Climate, and the like, ſhould be no better a motive to induce people from both places to populate it.

To which I anſwer, that whilſt it was under the *Dutch* Government, which hath been till within theſe ſix years.; there was little encouragement for any *Engliſh*, both in reſpect of their ſafety from the *Indians*, the *Dutch* being almoſt always in danger of them, and their *Bever*-trade not admitting of a War, which would have been deſtructive to their

trade,

trade, which was the main thing profecuted by the
Dutch. And fecondly, the *Dutch* gave fuch bad
Titles to Lands, together with their exacting of the
Tenths of all which men produced off their Land,
that did much hinder the populating of it; together
with that general diflike the *English* have of living
under another Government; but fince the reduce
ment of it the e is feveral Towns of a confiderable
greatnefs begun and fetled by people out of *New-
England*, and every day more and more come to
view and fett'e.

To give fome fatisfaction to people that fhall be
defirous to tranfport themfelves thither, (the Countrey being capable of entertaining many thoufands,)
how and after what manner people live, and how
Land may be procured, &c. I fhall anfwer, that the
ufual way, is for a Company of people to joyn to
together, either enough to make a Town, or a lef-
fer number; Thefe go with the confent of the Go-
vernor, and view a Tract of Land, there being choice
enough, and finding a place convenient for a Town,
they return to the Governour, who upon their defire admits them into the Colony, and gives them
a Grant or Patent for the faid Land, for themfelves
and Affociates. Thefe perfons being thus qualifi-
ed, fettle the place, and take in what inhabitants to
themfelves they fhall fee caufe to admit of, till their
Town be full; thefe Affociates thus taken in have
equal priviledges with themfelves, and they make a
divifion of the Land fuitable to every mans occaffons,
no man being debarr'd of fuch quantities as he hath
occafion for, the reft they let lie in common till they
have occafion for a new divifion, never dividing
their Pafture-land at all, which lies in common to
the whole Town. The beft Commodities for any,
to carry with them is Clothing, the Countrey being
full

full of all sorts of Cattel, which they may furnish themselves withal at an easie rate, for any sorts of *English* Goods; as likewise Instruments for Husbandry and Building, with Nails, Hinges, Glass, and the like; For the manner how they get a livelihood, it is principally by Corn and Cattel, which will there fetch them any Commodities; likewise they sowe store of Flax, which they make every one Cloth of for their own wearing, as also woollen Cloth, and Linsey-woolsey, and had they more Trademen amongst them, they would in a little time live without the help of any other Conntrey for their Clothing; For Tradesmen there is none but live happily there, as Carpenters, Blacksmiths, Masons, Tailors, Weavers, Shoomakers, Tanners, Brickmakers, and so any other Trade; them that have no Trade betake themselves to Husbandry, get Land of their own, and live exceeding well.

Thus have I briefly given you a Relation of *New-York*, with the places thereunto adoyning; In which, if I have err'd, it is principally in not giving it its due commendation; for besides those earthly blessings where it is stor'd, Heaven hath not been wanting to open his Treasure, in sending down seasonable showres upon the Earth, blessing it with a sweet and pleasant Air, and a Continuation of such Influences as tend to the Health both of Man and Beast: and the Climate hath such an affinity with that of *England*, that it breeds ordinarily no alteration to those which remove thither; that the name of seasoning, which is common to some other Countreys hath never there been known; That I may say, and say truly, that if there be any
terrestrial

terreſtria' happineſs to be had by people of all ranks,
eſpecially of an inferior rank, it muſt certainly be
here : here any one may furniſh himſelf with land,
and live rent-free, yea, with ſuch a quantity of
land, that he may weary himſelf with walking over
his fields of Corn, and all ſorts of Grain : and let his
ſtock of Cattel amount to ſome hundreds, he needs
not fear their want of paſture in the Summer, or
Fodder in the Winter, the Woods affording ſuffici-
ent ſupply. For the Summer-ſeaſon, where you
have graſs as high as a mans knees, nay, as high as
his wiſte, interlaced with Pea-vines and other weeds
that Cattel much delight in, as much as a man can
preſs thorough ; and theſe woods alſo every mile or
half-mile are furniſhed with freſh ponds, brooks,
or rivers, where all ſorts of Cattel, during the heat
of the day, do quench their thirſt and cool themſelves ; theſe brooks and rivers being invironed of
each ſide with ſeveral ſorts of trees and Grape-vines,
the Vines, Arbor-like, interchanging places and croſ-
ſing theſe rivers, does ſhade and ſhelter them from
the ſcorching beams of *Sols* fiery influence : Here
thoſe which Fortune hath frown'd upon in *England*,
to deny them an inheritance amongſt their Brethren,
or ſuch as by their utmoſt labors can ſcarcely procure a living, I ſay ſuch may procure here inherit-
ances of lands and poſſeſſions, ſtock themſelves with
all ſorts of Cattel, enjoy the benefit of them whilſt
they live, and leave them to the benefit of their children when they die : Here you need no trouble the
Shambles for meat, nor Bakers and Brewers for Beer
and Bread, nor run to a Linnen-Draper for a ſupply,
every one making *their* own Linnen, and a great part
of their woollen-cloth for their ordinary wearing :
And how prodigal, if I may ſo ſay, hath Nature been
to furniſh the Countrey with all ſorts of wilde Beaſts

and

and Fowle, which every one hath an interest in, and
may hunt at his pleasure; where besides the pleasure in hunting, he may furnish his house with excellent fat Venison, Turkies, Geese, Heath-Hens,
Cranes, Swans, Ducks, Pidgeons, and the like:
and wearied with that, he may go a Fishing, where
the Rivers are so furnished, that he may supply himself with Fish before he can leave off the Recreation:
Where you may travel by Land upon the same Con-
tinent hundreds of miles, and passe thorough Towns
and Villages, and never hear the least complaint for
want, nor hear any ask you for a farthing: there
you may lodge in the fields and woods, travel from
one end of the Countrey to another, with as much
security as if you were lockt within your own Cham-
ber; And if you chance to meet with an *Indian*-
Town, they shall give you the best entertainment
they have, and upon your desire, direct you on your
way: But that which adds happiness to all the rest,
is the Healthfulness of the place, where many people
in twenty years time never know what sickness is:
where they look upon it as a great mortality if two
or three die out of a town in a years time; where
besides the sweetness of the Air, the Countrey it self
sends forth such a fragrant smell, that it may be per-
ceived at Sea before they can make the Land: where
no evil fog or vapour doth no sooner appear, but a
North-west or Westerly winde doth immediately dis-
solve it, and drive it away: What shall I say more?
you shall scarce see a house, but the South-side is be-
girt with Hives of Bees, which increase after an in-
credible manner: That I must needs say, that if there
be any terrestrial *Canaan*, 'tis surely here, where the
Land floweth with milk and honey. The inhabitants
are blest with Peace and plenty, blessed in their Countrey, blessed in their Fields, blessed in the Fruit of

D
their

their bodies, in the fruit of their grounds, in the increase of their Cattel, Horses and Sheep, blessed in their Basket, and in their Store; In a word, blessed in whatsoever they take in hand, or go about, the Earth yielding plentiful increase to all their painful labours,

Were it not to avoid prolixity I could say a great deal more, and yet say too little, how free are those parts of the world from that pride and oppression, with their miserable effects, which many, nay almost all parts of the world are troubled, with being ignorant of that pomp and bravery which aspiring Humours are servants to, and striving after almost every where: where a Waggon or Cart gives as good content as a Coach, and a piece of their home-made Cloth, better then the finest Lawns or richest Silks: and though their low roofed houses may seem to shut their doors against pride and luxury, yet how do they stand wide open to let charity in and out, either to assist each other, or relieve a stranger, and the distance of place from other Nations, doth secure them from the envious frowns of ill-affected Neighbours, and the troubles which usually arise thence.

Now to conclude, its possible some may say, what needs a Relation of a place of so long standing as N. W. York hath been? In answer to which I have said something before, as to satisfie the desires of many that never had any Relation of it. Secondly, though it hath been long setled, yet but lately reduced to his Majesties obedience, and by that means but new or unknown to the English; Else certainly those great number of Furs, that have been lately transported from thence into Holland had never past the hands of our English Furriers: Thirdly, never any Relation before was published to my knowledge and
the

the place being capable of entertaining so great a number of inhabitants, where they may with Gods blessing, and their own industry, live as happily as any people in the world. A true Relation was necessary, not only for the encouragement of many that have a desire to remove themselves, but for the satisfaction of others that would make a trade thither.

FINIS.

The Accurate Accomptant or London-Merchant, Containing an Analysis for Instructions and Directions for a Methodical keeping Merchants Accompts, by way of Debitor and Creditor, very useful for all Merchants or other, that desire to learn or teach the Exact Method of keeping Merchants Accompts, by Thomas Brown Accomptant; To be sold by John Hancock, at the first shop in Popes Head Alley, at the sign of the Three Bibles in Cornhil, 1670.